Hans Werner Henze

Olly on the Shore

for solo piano (2001)

Chester Music

CH81004
ISBN 978-1-78305-020-8

Music setting by Robin Hagues

© 2001 Chester Music Ltd
Published in Great Britain by Chester Music Limited

Head office:
14–15, Berners Street,
London W1T 3LJ
England

Tel +44 (0)20 7612 7400
Fax +44 (0)20 7612 7549

Sales and hire:
Music Sales Distribution Centre,
Newmarket Road,
Bury St. Edmunds,
Suffolk IP33 3YB
England

Tel +44 (0)1284 702600
Fax +44 (0)1284 768301

www.musicsalesclassical.com

Hans Werner Henze
Olly on the Shore
(2001)

Vor langer Zeit, als ich noch ein Kind in der westfälischen Provinz war, kam mir der Titel (nicht die Musik und auch nicht der Text) „Molly on the Shore" in die Hände. Wer war diese Molly? Ich fragte mich das beständig (war sie eine Irin? Oder eine Schottin?), und wer war Mr Grainger, der Komponist? Viele Jahre später in London fand ich es heraus, als der fünfzigste Geburtstag meines Freundes Olly (Oliver Knussen) näher und näher rückte. Ich wollte für ihn ein Klavierstück mit dem besagten Titel schreiben (natürlich ohne den Anfangsbuchstaben M). Ich denke mit großer Zuneigung an ihn, wie er am Meerufer von Suffolk neben seinem wunderschönen Haus steht, wie er über den Ozean blickt, wie er wunderbare Welten aus zukünftigen Tönen und Rhythmen erspäht und herbeiruft, um die nächsten fünfzig Jahre seines Lebens zu füllen: Oliver Knussen, der brillante Kopf, der vornehme Mensch und der große Künstler.

© Hans Werner Henze
Marino, May 2002

Hans Werner Henze
Olly on the Shore
(2001)

A long time ago, when I was still a child back in provincial Westphalia, I came across the title (not the music, nor the lyrics) of "Molly on the Shore". Who was this Molly, I kept asking myself (was she Irish? or Scottish?), and who was Mr Grainger, the composer? I eventually found out, years later in London, as my friend Olly's (Oliver Knussen's) fiftieth birthday was approaching. I thought I'd write him a piano piece with the same title (except for the initial M). I think of him most affectionately, standing on the Suffolk shore near his lovely house, looking out across the ocean, looking and calling out to a world of wonderful images made of sounds and rhythms and tunes still to come, inspiring his work for the next fifty years: Oliver Knussen, the brilliant mind, the gentle man and the great artist.

© Hans Werner Henze
Marino, May 2002

The world premiere of Hans Werner Henze's *Olly on the Shore* took place on
1 July 2001 in La Leprara, Marino, Italy, given by Martin Zehn, piano, as part
of a birthday tribute concert for the composer's seventieth birthday.

Duration: *c*.2 minutes

A recording of *Olly on the Shore*, performed by Rolf Hind, is available on the
London Sinfonietta Label, Catalogue Number: SINFCD12004

In this score:

> ➤ An accidental applies only to the note it immediately precedes
> ➤ A tie is indicated by a horizontal line

Olly on the Shore *

(Twilight, a song for piano)

Hans Werner Henze
Arr. Martin Zehn

Andante cantabile, con moto

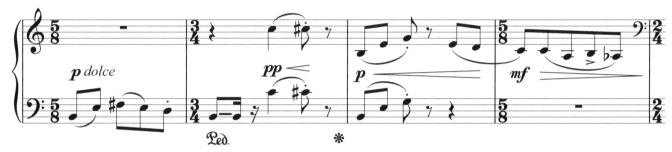

* (with apologies to Percy Grainger. *Molly on the Shore* is published by Schott & Co. Ltd, London)

Un poco meno mosso